Nelson English

Workbook 3

This book belongs to

_____

Sarah Lindsay and Wendy Wren

OXFORD UNIVERSITY PRESS

OXFORD
UNIVERSITY PRESS

Great Clarendon Street, Oxford, OX2 6DP, United Kingdom

Oxford University Press is a department of the University of Oxford.
It furthers the University's objective of excellence in research, scholarship,
and education by publishing worldwide. Oxford is a registered trade mark
of Oxford University Press in the UK and in certain other countries.

Text © Sarah Lindsay and Wendy Wren 2018
The moral rights of the author have been asserted.

First published 2018

All rights reserved. No part of this publication may be reproduced, stored in a retrieval system, or transmitted, in any form or by any means, without the prior permission in writing of Oxford University Press, or as expressly permitted by law, by licence or under terms agreed with the appropriate reprographics rights organization. Enquiries concerning reproduction outside the scope of the above should be sent to the Rights Department, Oxford University Press, at the address above.

You must not circulate this work in any other form
and you must impose this same condition on any acquirer.

British Library Cataloguing in Publication Data

Data available

ISBN: 978-0-1984-1990-7

9 10 8

Paper used in the production of this book is a natural, recyclable product made from wood grown in sustainable forests. The manufacturing process conforms to the environmental regulations of the country of origin.

Printed in China by Golden Cup

Acknowledgements
Series consultant: John Jackman

Cover and inside illustrations by Q2A Media Services Inc.

Page make-up by Aptara

The publisher and authors would like to thank the following for permission to use photographs and other copyright material:

p18, 13(bl), 67: Shutterstock.

Contents

Unit 1	A Home for Grandfather	4
Unit 2	Would You Like to Live Here?	8
Unit 3	The Princess and the Pea	12
Unit 4	Hans Christian Andersen	16
Unit 5	New Neighbours	20
Unit 6	Rabbits	24
Unit 7	A Contents Page	28
Unit 8	Animal Tales	32
Unit 9	The Maze Game	36
Unit 10	The Sound Collector	40
Unit 11	Staying Healthy	44
Unit 12	A Birthday Party	48
Unit 13	Book Reviews	52
Unit 14	Book Hunt	56
Unit 15	Sorry, Sorry, Sorry	60
Unit 16	All about Sport	64
Unit 17	Me and Mister P	68
	Glossary	72

UNIT 1 A Home for Grandfather

Vocabulary

Synonyms

A Draw a line to join each underlined word to its synonym.

1 a <u>dull</u> book   clever
2 his <u>big</u> eyes   dad
3 her <u>smart</u> brother   sad
4 my <u>father</u>   wealthy
5 a <u>rich</u> woman   large
6 her <u>miserable</u> face   boring

B Write a word that has the same meaning as the underlined word or phrase in each sentence.

1 William looked down the <u>street</u>.   _____
2 He noticed the removal <u>van</u>.   _____
3 William <u>watched</u> the men unload the van.   _____
4 He was upset about <u>moving out of</u> his room.   _____

Punctuation

Direct speech

> **Direct speech** is when we write words that someone has said. We put " at the beginning of the spoken words and " at the end of the spoken words.
>
> "There will hardly be room for him to move about!" said William's mother.
>
> "Why doesn't he get smaller furniture?" asked William.

A Add the missing **speech marks**.

1 Do you like your new room? asked William.
2 It's very nice, said Grandfather.
3 Don't you think there is too much furniture? asked William.
4 I like my furniture, said Grandfather.
5 I like my toys, said William.

4

Spelling

ing and ed endings

> To add **ing** to a word, look at the letter before the last letter.
> - If it is a consonant, add **ing** or **ed**.
>
> **Be careful!** When you add **ing** or **ed** to a word that ends in **e**, you need to remove the **e** and add **ing** or **ed**.
>
> - If it is a single vowel (a, e, i, o, u), double the last letter, then add **ing** or **ed**.
>
> **Be careful!** This rule doesn't work for words ending in **w**, **x** or **y**.
>
> - If there are two vowels before the last letter, just add **ing** or **ed**.

A Write what each word was before **ing** or **ed** was added. The first one has been done to help you.

1. driving — drive
2. baked — _____
3. smiling — _____
4. tipped — _____
5. shouted — _____
6. cooked — _____
7. grumbling — _____
8. chatted — _____
9. shopping — _____
10. clapping — _____
11. shaking — _____
12. swimming — _____
13. blowing — _____
14. liked — _____
15. listing — _____
16. planned — _____

B Choose four words ending in either **ing** or **ed** and use them in sentences of your own.

1. _____
2. _____
3. _____
4. _____

Grammar

Verb tenses

> Remind yourself of the following **verb tenses**.
>
> **present simple:** William **grumbles** about his new room.
> **present progressive:** William **is grumbling** about his new room.
> **past simple:** William **grumbled** about his new room.
> **past progressive:** William **was grumbling** about his new room.

A Underline the **past progressive verb** in each sentence.

1 William was playing with his model railway.
2 Grandfather was arriving this week.
3 The van was standing outside the house.
4 The men were moving the furniture.

B Copy the sentences.
Change the underlined verbs into the **past progressive tense**.

1 The van stood outside the house.
   _____

2 Grandfather's furniture arrived.
   _____

3 William ate his dinner.
   _____

C Complete these sentences with **past progressive verbs**.

1 I _____ _____ with a model railway.

2 They _____ _____ for Grandfather.

3 Mother _____ _____ dinner.

Settings

> Where a story takes place is called the **setting**.
> You need to describe the setting of a story very carefully so the reader can imagine where events are happening.

1. Imagine that you have made a den indoors or outside. Write words and phrases to describe your den.

   The walls   What are they made of?

   a Write some words you could use to describe the walls of your den:

   _____   _____   _____

   _____   _____   _____

   The roof   What is it made of?

   b Write some words you could use to describe the roof of your den:

   _____   _____   _____

   _____   _____   _____

   The door   What is it made of?

   c Write some words you could use to describe the door of your den:

   _____   _____   _____

   _____   _____   _____

2. Write some words or phrases you could use to describe how you feel when you are inside your den:

   _____   _____   _____

   _____   _____   _____

   _____   _____   _____

3. Use the words you have written to describe your den in sentences.

   _____

   _____

   _____

   _____

   _____

UNIT 2 Would You Like to Live Here?

Vocabulary

Alphabetical order

> The words in a dictionary are in **alphabetical order**. Words starting with *a* come first, words starting with *b* come second, and so on. Words starting with *z* come last.
>
> If the words begin with the same letter, you need to look at the second letter in each word.

A For each letter below, write down the letter that comes before it in the alphabet.

1 ___ c 2 ___ j 3 ___ s
4 ___ z 5 ___ g 6 ___ r

B Write each of these words in the order you would find them in a dictionary.

1 prize   palace   pudding   potato   pet

_____

2 thumb   tree   table   tube   telephone

_____

Punctuation

Capital letters and full stops

> A **sentence** starts with a **capital letter**.
> A **sentence** usually ends with a **full stop**.
>
> In some countries some people live in tents**.**

A 1 Write a **sentence** about your home.

_____

_____

2 Write a **sentence** about your school.

_____

_____

8

Spelling

Silent letters

> Some words have **silent letters** that we don't hear when we say the words aloud.
>
> **ch**aracter has a silent **h**   **sc**enery has a silent **c**
>
> Silent letters can make words tricky to spell.

A Sort these words into the table.

> write   scene   character   scent   chemist
> wrong   wrap   science   chaos

Words with a silent **h**	Words with a silent **w**	Words with a silent **c**

B Each of these words has a missing silent letter.

Write each word correctly. Check your spellings in a dictionary.

1 cemical _____   2 rist _____
3 sent _____   4 siencific _____
5 caracter _____   6 rong _____
7 senery _____   8 riting _____

C Each of these words has a silent letter. Circle the silent letter then write the word in a sentence.

1 t h u m b _____

2 y o u n g _____

3 k n o c k _____

4 k n o w _____

Grammar

Singular and plural

> We usually add **s** to a **naming word** when we mean **more than one**.
>
> If a noun ends with **s, x, ch** or **sh**, we add **es**.
>
> one tent   two tent**s**   one porch   two porch**es**
>
> When a noun ends in a **consonant + y**, we drop the **y** and add **ies**.
>
> one country   two countr**ies**
>
> When a noun ends in a **vowel + y**, just add **s**.
>
> one toy   two toy**s**

Remember, **singular** means one and **plural** means more than one.

A Write the **plural** of these nouns.

Put each **plural noun** into a sentence of your own.

1. berry   plural: _____

   Sentence: _____
   _____

2. hobby   plural: _____

   Sentence: _____
   _____

3. tray   plural: _____

   Sentence: _____
   _____

B Write the **singular** of these nouns.

Put each **singular noun** into a sentence of your own.

1. ponies   singular: _____

   Sentence: _____
   _____

2. keys   singular: _____

   Sentence: _____
   _____

3. lorries   singular: _____

   Sentence: _____
   _____

Fact and fiction

Use this page to write **facts** about your family.

How many people are in your family? _____

What are the names and ages of your brothers, if you have any?

_____
_____
_____

What are the names and ages of your sisters, if you have any?

_____
_____
_____

Who do you live with?

_____
_____
_____

What are they like?

_____
_____
_____

What languages do you speak at home?

_____
_____

What does your family enjoy doing?

_____
_____
_____
_____
_____
_____

UNIT 3 The Princess and the Pea

Vocabulary

Homophones

Remember, **homophones** are words that sound the same but are spelt differently and have different meanings.

A Complete each sentence with the correct homophone.

1 It was a wet and windy _____.   [night/knight]
2 The king _____ a knock at the door.   [herd/heard]
3 The prince wanted to _____ if the woman was a real princess.   [no/know]
4 The king asked the princess if she _____ like to come in.   [wood/would]

B Underline the homophones in these sentences.

1 I slipped and threw the ball through the window.
2 I could not undo the knot in my laces.

Punctuation

Apostrophes of contraction

Contractions are words that have been made smaller. An **apostrophe** is used in place of the missing letter or letters.

I am   I'm

This is an **apostrophe**: '.

A Write the words that make these **contractions**.

1 they're _____   2 we've _____
3 he's   _____   4 I've   _____
5 you're   _____   6 she's _____

B Write the **contractions** of these words.

1 he has   _____   2 we are _____
3 you have _____   4 I have _____
5 they have _____   6 it is   _____

Spelling

wa and qua words

A Find eight **wa** and **qua** words in the word search. Copy the words.

A	S	W	X	D	E	L	N	F
P	Q	U	A	N	T	I	T	Y
B	U	O	J	T	Y	Z	K	W
E	A	G	H	L	E	S	H	A
Q	L	S	Q	N	O	R	E	T
D	I	F	R	B	W	E	N	C
L	T	S	Q	U	A	S	H	H
Z	Y	W	I	V	S	W	A	N
V	W	A	R	M	P	O	S	R

_____ _____ _____ _____

_____ _____ _____ _____

B Match a word you have written above with each of these pictures.

1
_____

2
_____

3
_____

4
_____

5
_____

6
_____

C Write each of these words in a sentence.

quality _____

_____

quantity _____

_____

You can use a dictionary to help you.

13

Grammar

Conjunctions

> **Conjunctions** are words we use to join sentences.
> These are useful **conjunctions** that have to do with **time**.
>
> when   while   before   after
>
> The prince was very sad **when** he returned home.
> The king heard a knock **while** he was going upstairs.
> The princess arrived **before** the prince had gone to bed.
> Things would seem better **after** the prince had a good night's sleep.

A Underline the **conjunction** in each sentence.

1 I read the story before I answered the questions.

2 The prince will marry after he meets a real princess.

3 The king talked to the young lady while the prince came down the stairs.

4 I put my books away when I finished my homework.

B Join each pair of sentences with a **conjunction** from the box.
Use each one only once.

| when | but | before | because | and |

1 I found the book.　　　　I read the story.

_____

2 I didn't finish the story.　　I lost the book.

_____

3 I went to sleep.　　　　I had finished the story.

_____

4 I finished the book.　　　I took it back to the library.

_____

5 I liked that story.　　　　I didn't like the other one.

_____

Writing

Play scripts

1 Read this picture story.

2 Finish writing the story as a play script. Start in the space below, and continue in your exercise book.

Characters:	What they say and do:
Leo	(Gloomily) I think we're lost, Raj.
Raj	
____	
____	
____	
____	
____	

UNIT 4 Hans Christian Andersen

Vocabulary

Root words

> A **root word** is a word to which prefixes can be added (to the beginning) or suffixes can be added (to the end) to make other words in the same family.

A See how many words you can make from each root word below. Choose prefixes and suffixes from the box. The first one has been done to help you.

> **Prefixes**
> un   re   im
>
> **Suffixes**
> s   er   ing   ed   ly   ion   est   ness

1. happy — unhappy   unhappily   happier   happily   happiest   happiness
2. mark _____
3. tall _____
4. invent _____
5. perfect _____

B Choose one of the root words from **Activity A**. Make up a sentence using as many of its family words as you can. For example:
The inventor invented an invention to invent inventions.

_____
_____

Punctuation

Apostrophes of possession

This is an apostrophe: **'** .

> **Possessive nouns** tell you who **owns** something. They have an **apostrophe** and an **s** at the end.
>
> Andersen**'s** story is called 'The Little Mermaid'.
> Andersen's story = the story belonging to Anderson

The first one is done for you.

A Rewrite these phrases using an **apostrophe**.

1. the story belonging to the child — the child's story
2. the pupil belonging to the school _____
3. the book belonging to the author _____
4. the fame belonging to Andersen _____
5. the son belonging to the king _____

Spelling

Soft c words

Say the word **princess** aloud.

'The Pri**c**ess and the Pea'

The **c** in pri**c**ess is called a **soft c**. It sounds more like an **s**!

A Match the clues with a **soft c** word from the box.

| cylinder | city | centre |
| spicy | pencil | entrance |

Say the words aloud. That will help you!

1 found in the middle _____

2 a shape _____

3 the way in _____

4 you write or draw with it _____

5 a busy place where people live and work _____

6 something with lots of flavour _____

B Circle the letter that follows the **soft c** in each word in **Activity A**.

Which three letters usually follow the **soft c**? ___ ___ ___

C Write three **soft c** words with each of these letter patterns. Don't use words already found on this page!

ce   **ci**   **cy**

_____   _____   _____

_____   _____   _____

_____   _____   _____

Grammar

Verbs: irregular past simple tense

> To put a **verb** into the **past simple tense**, we usually add **ed** or **d** to the verb family name.
>
> | Verb family name | Past simple tense |
> |---|---|
> | to publish | publish**ed** |
> | to live | live**d** |
>
> Some **verbs** do not follow this rule.
>
> | | |
> |---|---|
> | to write | wrote |
> | to make | made |
> | to begin | began |

A Underline the **past simple verb** in each sentence.

1 I enjoyed the story of 'The Princess and the Pea'.

2 The author's stories became very popular.

3 She drew a picture of the Snow Queen.

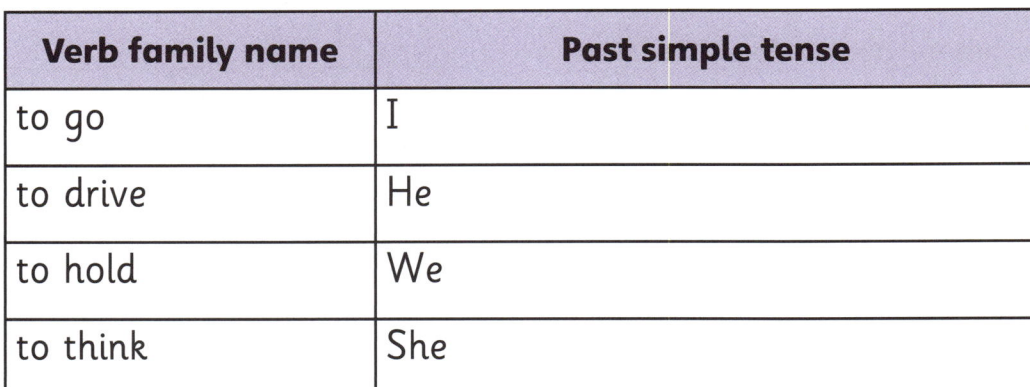

B Complete the table

Verb family name	Past simple tense
to go	I
to drive	He
to hold	We
to think	She

C Use these **past simple verbs** in sentences of your own.

1 found _____

_____

2 grew _____

_____

3 spoke _____

_____

Key words and phrases

The activities in this section focus on writing full sentences using **key words and phrases**.

1 These key words or phrases are from a book about J. M. Barrie, who wrote the well-known story *Peter Pan*. Use each set of key words to write a sentence about J. M. Barrie.

a | born 1860   died 1937

_____

_____

b | born Scotland

_____

_____

c | father – David   mother – Margaret

_____

_____

d | father a weaver

_____

_____

e | 1883–1890 journalist in Nottingham and then London, England

_____

_____

f | *Peter Pan*, play, first performed 1904

_____

_____

UNIT 5 New Neighbours

Vocabulary

Synonyms for said

When you are writing dialogue (what people said), you don't have to keep repeating **said**. There are lots of other words you can use instead.

"I miss our old house," **complained** Alex.
"I miss our old house," **grumbled** Alex.

Remember, the **synonym** of a word is a word that has the same or a very similar meaning.

A Write a list of six synonyms you could use instead of the word **said**.

_____   _____   _____

_____   _____   _____

B Choose three of the words you have written and include them in your own sentences. Don't forget the speech marks!

1 _____

2 _____

3 _____

Punctuation

Direct speech

Direct speech is when we write words that someone has said in speech marks.
   "I miss our old house," said Alex.
Sometimes the **speaker's name** comes before the spoken words.
   Alex said, "I miss our old house."
We use a **comma** to separate the non-spoken and spoken words.

A Copy and punctuate these **direct speech** sentences.

1 Rose said We are your new neighbours

_____

2 We should make them feel welcome said Father Mouse

_____

3 Shall we invite them for tea asked Mother Mouse

_____

Spelling

ly word endings

A **suffix** is added to the end of a word to slightly change its meaning. The **ly** suffix starts with a consonant letter so it is simply added straight to the root word.

careful + **ly** = careful**ly**

If **ly** is added to words ending in **y**, we change the **y** to an **i** before adding **ly**.

happy + **ly** = happ**ily**

A Complete these word sums.

1 week + ly = _____
2 urgent + ly = _____
3 wonderful + ly = _____
4 usual + ly = _____
5 angry + ly = _____
6 complete + ly = _____
7 like + ly = _____
8 pretty + ly = _____
9 heavy + ly = _____
10 grateful + ly = _____

B Can you find a **ly** word to go with each of these letters in the alphabet? Use a dictionary to help you.

You won't find a word for every letter!

a _____ b _____
c _____ d _____
e _____ f _____
g _____ h _____
i _____ j _____
k ___kindly___ l _____
m _____ n _____
o _____ p _____
q _____ r _____
s _____ t _____
u _____ v _____
w _____ x _____
y _____ z _____

21

Grammar

Articles

> The words **a** and **an** are called **articles**.
> We use **a** before words beginning with a consonant.
>   **a** house   **a** family   **a** shoe
> We use **an** before words beginning with a vowel.
>   **an** egg   **an** animal   **an** orange

A Write **a** or **an** before each word.

1. _____ insect
2. _____ door
3. _____ ice-cream
4. _____ apple
5. _____ frog
6. _____ elephant

B In some of these sentences, **a** and **an** are used incorrectly. Put a **cross** against the incorrect sentences.

- a I had an lovely ice cream. ☐
- b May I have an orange? ☐
- c We read an story about a family of mice. ☐
- d A ant bit me! ☐
- e I've lost a shoe! ☐

C Copy and **correct** the sentences that are incorrect.

_____
_____
_____
_____

Writing

Settings and dialogue

Use this page to practise describing a setting and writing dialogue.

1. Colour the picture.

2. Write some words to describe each of the items in the picture.

The slides	The colours	The whole playground

3. Write down what you would say to your teacher if you went on a school trip to this place. Remember to put the spoken words in speech marks.

_____

_____

_____

UNIT 6 Rabbits

Vocabulary

Using a dictionary

A **dictionary** is very useful for checking how to spell words. It also gives the meanings, or **definitions**, of words.

A Use a dictionary to help you choose the best definition for each word. Draw a line between each word and the correct definition.

1 **annoy**
    a a type of glue
    b to make someone cross
    c to be very sorry

2 **fable**
    a a short story with a meaning
    b weak
    c a type of flower

3 **obedient**
    a to be naughty
    b a small animal
    c willing to obey

4 **hay**
    a bread
    b to shout loudly
    c cut grass that is used to feed animals

B Use each word from **Activity A** in a sentence of your own.

1 _____

2 _____

3 _____

4 _____

Punctuation

Capital letters, question marks and exclamation marks

All **sentences** start with a **capital letter**.
A **statement** ends with a **full stop**.
A **question** ends with a **question mark**.
An **exclamation** ends with an **exclamation mark**.

A Complete each sentence with a **full stop**, **question mark** or **exclamation mark**.

1. The rabbit has escaped
2. Where has it gone
3. We must find it before it gets dark
4. Shall we ask Dad to help us

Spelling

Soft g words

The letter **j** is never used at the end of English words. The sound is made by a **soft g** using **ge** or **dge**.

Wild rabbits often live in lar**ge** groups.

Remember, when we add **ing** to a word ending in **e**, we drop the **e** and add **ing**.

jud**ge** + **ing** = jud**ging**

A Add **ge** or **dge** to each of these words. Then write the word you have made in a sentence.

1. gara____ _____

2. bri____ _____

3. pa____ _____

4. he____ _____

25

B Complete the sentences by selecting a word from the word box and adding **ing**.

| arrange | change | challenge | stage |

1 The test was very _____!
2 Our school will be _____ a play.
3 I think the weather is _____.
4 My mum is _____ a surprise for my brother.

C Write a definition for each word. Use a dictionary if you need to.

1 knowledge _____

2 voyage _____

3 advantage _____

4 luggage _____

Grammar

Prepositions

A **preposition** is a word that shows the relationship of a **noun** or **pronoun** to another word in the sentence.

Pet rabbits are usually kept **in** wooden hutches.

Pet rabbits exercise **outside** the hutch.

A Write all of the **prepositions** from the box that can follow each word below.

Some **prepositions** will go with more than one word.

| up | on | after | at |
| over | behind | in | down |

1 jump _____   2 sit _____

3 get _____   4 come _____

5 hide _____   6 look _____

B Use each of these **prepositions** in sentences of your own.

1 between _____

_____

2 through _____

_____

3 towards _____

_____

4 around _____

_____

Writing

Simple reports

1 You are going to write a **simple report** about a pet animal of your choice. Use this page to help you plan your report.

   a What animal are you going to write about? _____

   b Write some notes about:

   - where the animal lives/sleeps: _____

   _____

   _____

   _____

   _____

   - what the animal eats: _____

   _____

   _____

   _____

   _____

   - how to look after the animal: _____

   _____

   _____

   _____

   _____

2 Use your notes to write a report about the animal in your exercise book.

UNIT 7 A Contents Page

Vocabulary

Using a thesaurus

> Remember, **synonyms** are words with similar meanings. An **antonym** means the opposite.

A thesaurus is a book that gives the **synonyms** of common words in alphabetical order.
For each word, there is a list of synonyms and the **antonym**, if it has one.

antonym   synonyms

cold (hot) cool, chilly, frosty, icy, wintry, arctic
come (go) arrive, appear, reach, approach, enter, advance
correct (incorrect) right, exact, true, proper, accurate

A Copy these sentences. Replace the underlined words with ones that have a similar meaning. Use the thesaurus entries above to help you.

1 There is a <u>cold</u> wind today.

2 The forecast says that the storm will <u>come</u> here soon.

3 Weather forecasts aren't always <u>correct</u>.

When we write a **list** in a sentence we use **commas** between the items in the list. We can join the last two things in the list with **and**, **but** and **or**.

Punctuation

Commas in lists

> Remember your **commas**!

A Write sentences of your own including these **lists**.

1   rain   fog   hail

2   sun   wind   thunder

Spelling

sion word ending

The word ending **ion** is a very common **suffix**. It is added to many root words.
The suffix **ion** always has either a **t** or an **s** in front of it.
This unit covers the suffix with an **s** in front of it.

The teacher made a good deci**sion**.

A Look carefully at the end of these words. Sort the words into the table according to their endings.

You could look up the meaning of the words in a dictionary.

vision	confusion	session	conclusion
division	possession	evasion	occasion
persuasion	television	permission	inclusion

asion	ision	usion	ssion

B Draw a line to match the words with the correct definitions.

1 **permission** — something that you decide when you have thought about all the information connected with the situation

2 **confusion** — convincing someone to do something even though they may not want to

3 **persuasion** — allowing something to happen

4 **conclusion** — not being sure about what is happening or what something means

C Complete the sentences below with the correct word from **Activity B**.

1 My father gave me _____ to attend the school trip.

2 My friend didn't want to come, so I had to use some _____!

3 There was some _____ over where to meet.

4 The _____ was that we should meet in front of the school gate.

Grammar

Verbs: future tense

> **Verbs** tell us **what** happens.
> A verb **tense** tells us **when** something happens.
>
> present simple: It **rains**. present progressive: It **is raining**.
> past simple: It **rained**. past progressive: It **was raining**.
>
> If we want to write about what is **going to happen** we use the **future tense**.
>
> It **will rain** tomorrow. I **shall take** my umbrella.
>
> The **future tense** is made up of two parts:
> 1 **shall** after **I** and **we**
>   **will** after **you, he, she, it, they** and sometimes **I** and **we**
> 2 the **verb family name**.

A Change the present tense verb in each sentence into the **future tense**.

1 He looks for his umbrella.

   _____

2 The forecast tells us about the weather.

   _____

3 I wait for the rain to stop.

   _____

4 We are getting wet!

   _____

B Fill in the missing **verbs**.

Verb family name	Present simple tense	Past simple tense	Future tense
to rain	It rains	It _____	It _____ _____
to write	I _____	I wrote	I _____ _____
to thunder	It _____	It _____	It _____ _____
to forecast	He _____	He _____	He _____ _____

Contents page

1. You are going to write the **contents page** for an imaginary book. Use this page to plan your contents page.

   a What topic have you chosen? _____

   b Think of a title for your book: _____

2. Use the framework below to help you plan your contents page.

CONTENTS

	Page
_____	_____
_____	_____
_____	_____
_____	_____
_____	_____
_____	_____
_____	_____
_____	_____
_____	_____

UNIT 8 Animal Tales

Vocabulary

Alphabetical order

> It is important to know the order of the letters in the alphabet.

A The table below gives a code for the letters of the alphabet. Look at the table, and then write the sentence in code.

A	B	C	D	E	F	G	H	I	J	K	L	M
1	2	3	4	5	6	7	8	9	10	11	12	13

N	O	P	Q	R	S	T	U	V	W	X	Y	Z
14	15	16	17	18	19	20	21	22	23	24	25	26

The crab saw an old woman sitting on a log.

_____

B Write words or letters to answer these questions.

1 Which two letters are closest to the centre of the alphabet? _____

2 A is the first letter. Where do the other vowels come? _____

_____

Punctuation

Direct speech

> **Direct speech** is when we write words that someone has said. We can put the **speaker's name** or the **speaker's pronoun** (he/she) before the spoken words.
>
> **She said to the kind crab,** "You are a good, kind crab so I will do something for you now."
>
> We use a **comma** to separate the non-spoken and spoken words.

A Write endings of your choice to complete these direct speech sentences.

Remember to include the correct punctuation.

1 I said _____

2 My friend said _____

3 My teacher said _____

Spelling

er and est word endings

> A thing can be big**er** or small**er** than **one** other thing.
>
> The mouse is small**er** than an elephant.
>
> A thing can be the big**gest** or small**est** of **three or more** things.
>
> The mouse is the small**est** animal in the story.
>
> If a comparing word ends with **y**, we change the **y** to **i** before adding **er** or **est**.
>
> hap**py**   happ**ier**   happ**iest**

A Use the words in brackets to complete each sentence using the correct **er** or **est** ending.

1. The elephant is ____bigger____ than the mouse. [big]
2. The mouse is _____ than the hippo. [small]
3. The mouse is the _____ animal in the story. [clever]
4. The hippo said he was the _____ animal in the world. [strong]

 The first one is done for you.

B Complete this table.

Adjective	+er	+est
large		
funny		
hot		
sunny		
tall		
happy		
bright		

Grammar

Adjectives: comparatives and superlatives

Adjectives are describing words.

They tell us more about people, animals, places and things.

Adjectives that describe the **difference** between **two things** are **comparative** adjectives.

"I am **stronger** than you," said Mouse.

Adjectives that describe the **difference** between **three or more things** are **superlative** adjectives.

"I am the **strongest** animal in the world," said Hippo.

Some long adjectives make their **comparative** with **more** and their **superlative** with **most**.

more comfortable   **most** comfortable

A Complete the table with the missing **adjectives**

Adjective	Comparative	Superlative
old	older	
beautiful		most beautiful
bright		brightest
special	more special	
surprising		

B Use these **comparative** and **superlative adjectives** in sentences of your own.

1 more important _____

2 most exciting _____

3 more expensive _____

4 most interesting _____

Writing

Story beginnings

You are going to write the beginning of a story about an animal that is kind to an old lady who has hidden powers. You could begin your story in three ways:

1 by describing the setting
2 by describing the characters
3 with a conversation.

Write down ideas for each type of beginning.

1 Describing the setting

One day, an old lady was sitting and thinking.

Write some sentences to describe where the old lady was sitting.

_____
_____
_____
_____

2 Describing the characters

Once, there was a very old lady.

Write some more sentences to describe the old lady.

_____
_____
_____
_____

3 A conversation

"Good morning," said the frog to the old lady.

Write some more sentences to show what the frog and the old lady talked about.

_____
_____
_____
_____
_____

UNIT 9 The Maze Game

Vocabulary

Definitions

Some words are spelt the same but have more than one meaning. Below is an entry in a dictionary. If a word has two or more different **definitions**, they are numbered.

operate v (1) to run a machine (2) to repair a part of a person's body

operation n when surgeons repair part of an injured or ill person's body

operator n a person who runs a machine

→ definitions

A Write your own **definition** for each of these words and then check your answer in a dictionary.

1 edge _____

2 centre _____

3 way _____

Punctuation

Apostrophes of possession

Possessive nouns tell you who **owns** something. They have an **apostrophe** and an **s** at the end.

each **player's** playing piece = the playing piece belonging to each player

This is an **apostrophe**: '.

A Write these using an **apostrophe**.

1 the box belonging to the game _____

2 the centre belonging to the maze _____

3 the card belonging to the player _____

Spelling

tion word endings

> The **ending** or **suffix ion** is very common.
> The suffix **ion** always has either a **t** or an **s** in front of it.
> This unit covers the suffix with a **t** in front of it.
>
> When you get to a junc**tion**, spin the spinner to see which way to turn.

A Look carefully at the end of these words, then sort them into the table according to their endings.

position	station	lotion	fiction
direction	motion	celebration	fraction
addition	emotion	relation	competition

ation	tion	otion	ction

B Add the correct **tion** ending to these words.

1 instru_____   2 descrip_____

3 celebr_____   4 fi_____

5 st_____   6 rel_____

7 addi_____   8 se_____

C Check the words you have written in **Activity B** in a dictionary.
Rewrite any words you spelt wrong.

_____

_____

_____

Grammar

Word families

The four most important **parts of speech** are:

- **nouns** – naming words
- **verbs** – doing or being words
- **adjectives** – words that describe nouns
- **adverbs** – words that describe verbs.

Many words can be altered by adding or taking away **prefixes** and **suffixes** to create different parts of speech.
Words that are formed from the same **root word** are called **word families**.

We got great **enjoyment** from the game.	noun
The game was very **enjoyable**.	adjective
Did you **enjoy** the game?	verb
We played **enjoyably** all afternoon.	adverb

A Write the words in the box under the correct heading.

highest	quickly	squares	take
fewer	game	again	played
exact	dice	scored	firstly

Noun	Adjective	Verb	Adverb

B Complete the word webs with any words from the same word family that you can think of.

1   helped   helpful

   | help |

   _____ _____

2   agreement   disagree

   | agree |

   _____ _____

3   playful   _____

   | play |

   _____ _____

4   _____   _____

   | happy |

   _____ _____

Rules

You are going to write a list of **rules**. Use this page to help you.

1 What are you going to write rules for?
   - crossing the road ☐
   - cooking in the kitchen ☐
   - looking after a pet ☐

2 Now write your rules in the box with a reason for each one.

DO
Rule 1
Do _____
Reason: _____
_____
Rule 2
Do _____
Reason: _____
_____
Rule 3
Do _____
Reason: _____
_____

DON'T
Rule 1
Don't _____
Reason: _____
_____
Rule 2
Don't _____
Reason: _____
_____
Rule 3
Don't _____
Reason: _____
_____

UNIT 10 The Sound Collector

Vocabulary

Using a thesaurus

Remember, a **thesaurus** gives the **synonyms** of words in alphabetical order. For each word, there is a list of synonyms, and the **antonym**, if it has one.

Remember, **synonyms** are words with similar meanings. An **antonym** means the opposite.

A Write one **synonym** for the underlined word in each sentence. Use a thesaurus to help you.

1 I carried some books for my teacher to be <u>helpful</u>.

_____

2 She was <u>happy</u> to have some help.

_____

3 There were a lot of books and they were very <u>heavy</u>.

_____

B Write an **antonym** for each of the underlined words in **Activity A**.

1 _____

2 _____

3 _____

Punctuation

Apostrophes of possession

Remember, **possessive nouns** tell you who **owns** something.
Plural possessive nouns that end in **s** have an **apostrophe** at the end.

   the raindrops' drumming = the drumming belonging to the raindrops

Plural possessive nouns that do not end in **s** have an **apostrophe** and an **s** at the end.

   the children's voices = the voices belonging to the children

A Write these using an **apostrophe**.

1 the paws belonging to the kittens   _____

2 the windows belonging to the houses   _____

40

Spelling

ous word endings

> **ous** is an important word ending.
> If a word ends in **y** (that sounds like **ee** as in 'bee'), change the **y** to **i** before adding **ous**.
>
> 'The Sound Collector' is written by a fam**ous** poet. He has written var**ious** poems that make us think differently about everyday things.

A Complete these word sums.

1. fam + ous _____

   marvell + ous _____

   jeal + ous _____

2. var + ious _____

   fur + ious _____

   ser + ious _____

3. hid + eous _____

   court + eous _____

   outrag + eous _____

B Write a **definition** for each of these words. Use a dictionary to help you.

1. glamorous _____
2. victorious _____
3. dangerous _____
4. serious _____
5. courageous _____

C Choose three words from **Activity B** and write them in a sentence.

_____
_____
_____

Grammar

Abstract nouns

Most **nouns** are the names of things you can see and touch.

common noun   apple
proper noun   Taj Mahal
compound noun   football

Abstract nouns are the names of things you cannot touch, taste, smell or hear.

Here are some examples of abstract nouns:

Qualities	bravery	kindness	silence
Feelings	fear	sadness	happiness
Times	morning	evening	holiday

A   Write each **noun** from the box under the correct heading.

London	laughter	raindrop	night
silence	kitten	Everest	guilt
window	Africa	joy	pity

Some common nouns and compound nouns can also be concrete nouns.

Concrete nouns	Abstract nouns

B   Use these **abstract nouns** in sentences of your own.

1   brightness _____

_____

2   wisdom _____

_____

3   happiness _____

_____

4   pleasure _____

_____

Writing

Poems with sound words

You are going to write a poem using rhyme and **sound words**.

1

   a Make a list of six items that make a sound.

     _____   _____

     _____   _____

     _____   _____

feet on the street

   b Find a rhyming word for each item.

     _____   _____

     _____   _____

     _____   _____

a cat in a hat

   c Think of a sound word to describe the noise each item makes.

     _____   _____

     _____   _____

     _____   _____

a frog on a log

2 Match up the sound words with the items to create a line for your poem in each case.

_____

_____

_____

_____

_____

_____

3 Write a final copy of your poem in your exercise book.

UNIT 11 Staying Healthy

Vocabulary

Antonyms

> **Antonyms** are words that have opposite meanings.
>   **dirty** and **clean** are antonyms
>   **wet** and **dry** are antonyms
>
> Antonyms are sometimes created by adding the prefix **un** or **dis**.
>   trust   **dis**trust

A Use **un** or **dis** to make the **antonym** of each word.

1 pack _____   2 lock _____

3 important _____   4 agree _____

5 connect _____   6 certain _____

B Use three antonyms from **Activity A** in your own sentences.

_____

_____

_____

Punctuation

Apostrophes of contraction with not

This is an **apostrophe**: '.

> **Contractions** are words that have been made smaller.
> A letter or more than one letter is left out.
> An **apostrophe** is used in place of the missing letter or letters.
> We often use contractions with words with **not**.
>   cannot   can't

A Change the underlined words in each sentence into a **contraction**.

1 <u>Do not</u> eat before you wash your hands.   _____

2 I <u>would not</u> like to swallow germs!   _____

3 I <u>did not</u> know germs were everywhere!   _____

4 I <u>cannot</u> see any germs.   _____

Spelling

ou sounds

Some letter patterns have more than one sound. The **ou** letter pattern can make different sounds in different words. This unit looks at two of these sounds.

fo**u**nd   to**u**ch

A Write a word from the box to match each picture.

double	country	young	house
trouble	cloud	touch	mouse

1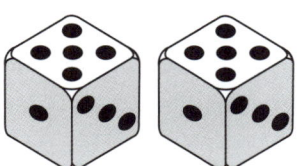

_____

2

_____

3

_____

4

_____

5

_____

6

_____

B Group together the words in **Activity A** that have the same **ou** sound.

Saying the words aloud will help you to hear the sound.

1 _____

2 _____

C With a line, link the words that have the same **ou** sound.

1 would   group

2 soup   sound

3 double   could

4 found   trouble

45

Grammar

Conjunctions

> **Conjunctions** are words that are used to join sentences. Here are some common conjunctions that you may know:
>
>   and   but   or   so   because
>
> Here are some other useful **conjunctions** to do with **time**.
>   Germs get on your hands **when** you touch something.
>   Keep washing your hands **while** you are cooking.
>   Wash your hands **before** you eat.
>   Wash your hands **after** playing with your pet.

A Underline the **conjunction** in each sentence.
1. The boys played outside before going home for lunch.
2. You must keep your hands clean because germs are everywhere.
3. I clean my teeth after I have eaten.

B Copy and join each pair of sentences using a **conjunction**.
1. The cook washed her hands. She had picked vegetables in the garden.

   _____
   _____

2. The cook kept washing her hands. She was cooking.

   _____
   _____

C Use these **conjunctions** in sentences of your own.
1. when

   _____
   _____

2. while

   _____
   _____

3. before

   _____
   _____

4. after

   _____
   _____

Writing

Flow diagrams

Use this page to complete a flow diagram showing the life cycle of a chicken.

1 The stages below are in the wrong order. Number them in the correct order.

After a while an egg hatches. _____

First the chicken lays her eggs. _____

The chick grows into an adult chicken. _____

The small chick grows quickly. _____

2 Use the information to complete your flow diagram.

What happens first?

_____

_____

What happens next?

_____

_____

What happens next?

_____

_____

What happens next?

_____

_____

UNIT 12 A Birthday Party

Vocabulary

Common expressions

> **Thank you** is an **expression** we use when someone has been kind or helpful.
>
> **Thank you** for the wonderful game you sent me.

A Complete the sentences, using the best expression from the box.

> I'm sorry   be careful   watch out   be quiet   excuse me

1 _____ , where is my classroom?

2 _____ , I lost your book.

3 _____ , there's a car coming!

B Use these expressions in sentences of your own.

1 thank you _____

2 I'm sorry _____

3 be careful _____

Punctuation

Apostrophes of contraction

> **Contractions** are words that have been made smaller. A letter or more than one letter is left out.
> An **apostrophe** is used in place of the missing letter or letters.
> did not   didn't

This is an **apostrophe**: '.

A Use these **contractions** in sentences of your own.

1 let's _____

2 won't _____

3 don't _____

Spelling

wh and **ph** words

> Many words that begin with **wh** are question words.
>   **Wh**at time is your party, Claire?
> Words with **ph** can be tricky to spell. The **ph** makes an **f** sound.
>   **ph**oto   al**ph**abet

A Write five questions of your own, each starting with a different **wh** word.

1 _____
2 _____
3 _____
4 _____
5 _____

B Match the words in the word box with these pictures.

| elephant | photo | whale |
| dolphin | phone | whiskers |

1
_____

2
_____

3
_____

4
_____

5
_____

6
_____

C Can you use **all** the words from **Activity B** in two sentences?

1 _____
2 _____

49

Grammar

Verbs: present perfect tense

> These are the **past tenses** that have been covered so far:
>
> **past simple:** Dad **made** a treasure hunt.
> **past continuous:** We **were playing** a game.
>
> We make the **present perfect tense** of **regular** verbs like this:
> **present simple** of the verb **to have** + the **ed** form of a verb.
>
> I **have saved** a piece of cake for you.
>
> Some verbs have **irregular** present perfect forms.
>
> My friends **have eaten** the rest of the cake.

A Copy the sentences. Change the underlined present simple verbs into the **present perfect tense**.

1 I <u>play</u> games at my birthday party.

_____

2 My grandmother <u>bakes</u> cakes for my birthday.

_____

3 I <u>open</u> my birthday presents.

_____

B Complete the table.

Verb family name	Past simple tense	Present perfect tense
to talk	I talked	I have talked
to invite	we _____	we _____
to enjoy	they _____	they _____
to call	she _____	she _____

C Use these **present perfect tense** verbs in sentences of your own.

1 she has visited _____

_____

2 he has collected _____

_____

Writing

A letter

Use this page to help you write a **letter** to a friend or relative, inviting them to stay with you.

Your address →

Date →

Name of the person you are writing to ↓

Dear _____

Your first paragraph, saying why you are writing the letter

Your second paragraph, saying what you will do if they come

Your third paragraph, saying you hope they can come

← Your friendly ending

← Your name

UNIT 13 Book Reviews

Vocabulary

Homonyms

> **Homonyms** are words that sound the same and are spelt the same, but which have different meanings.
> **Book** reviews help us choose what to read.
> Mum went online to **book** our cinema tickets.

A Circle the homonyms.

bank   island   fans   match   zoo   bark

nurse   atlas   sky   tale   watch

B Choose two homonyms from **Activity A**. Use each word in two sentences, to show the different meanings.

1 _____
_____

2 _____
_____

Punctuation

Capital letters, question marks and exclamation marks

> All **sentences** start with a **capital letter**.
> A **statement** ends with a **full stop**.
>   Maya faces many adventures.
> A **question** ends with a **question mark**.
>   Can Maya succeed in her quest?
> An **exclamation** ends with an **exclamation mark**.
>   It has disappeared!

A Complete each sentence with a **full stop**, **question mark** or **exclamation mark**.

1 Which book are you reading____

2 I am reading *Kenyan Adventure*____

3 That was the best book I've ever read____

Spelling

sure and ture endings

> The **ure** spelling pattern is usually found with the **sure** and **ture** word endings.
>
> Kenyan Adven**ture** is a plea**sure** to read

| furniture | measure | adventure | nature | treasure | signature |

A Match a word from the word box with each of these pictures.

1. treasure
2. measure
3. furniture
4. adventure
5. signature
6. nature

B Complete each of these words with **sure** or **ture**.

> Look up spellings or word meanings that you don't know in a dictionary.

1. mea_____ 2. pres_____ 3. mix_____

4. adven_____ 5. sculp_____ 6. struc_____

7. fu_____ 8. plea_____ 9. crea_____

C Write a definition for four of the words in **Activity B**.

1. _____
2. _____
3. _____
4. _____

Grammar

Paragraphing

> A **paragraph** is a group of sentences about **one main idea**. We begin a **new paragraph** when we write about **a different aspect** of a topic. We show a **new paragraph** has started by starting a new line.
>
> In the review of the book *The Mystery of the Vanishing House*, there are **four paragraphs**. Here is a summary of what each paragraph is about:
>
> paragraph 1: What the characters, Peter and his friends, usually do every Saturday
>
> paragraph 2: What was different on one Saturday morning
>
> paragraph 3: Solving the mystery of the vanishing house
>
> paragraph 4: Who would like to read the book

A If the reviewer had written more in the review of *The Mystery of the Vanishing House*, in which **paragraph** would she have put the following information?

Information	Paragraph
1 Peter and his friends cannot believe the house has vanished.	_____
2 If you have enjoyed books by the same author, you will love this book.	_____
3 Peter asks their neighbours who lived in the house.	_____
4 The children played hide and seek among the trees.	_____

B Sort the following sentences into two paragraphs.

Number the sentences **1** or **2** to show which paragraph they should go in. The first one has been done to help you.

I read a review about *The Mystery of the Vanishing House*. __1__

I'm really interested in animals so I think I will like this book. _____

The reviewer described how a house disappears and the characters try to find out why. _____

I read a review about *Kenyan Adventure* and Maya's quest to save a lion cub. _____

I would like to read this book because I like mystery stories. _____

The reviewer said that Maya has many adventures. _____

Book review

Use this page to help you structure a **book review**. Write the review about a book you have recently read.

Title: _____

Author: _____

The story is about _____

_____

_____

_____

_____

_____

It is set in _____

_____

_____

_____

_____

_____

One of the characters is _____

_____

_____

_____

_____

_____

My opinion of the story is _____

_____

_____

_____

_____

UNIT 14 Book Hunt

Vocabulary

Compound words

> **Compound words** can be made when two smaller words are added together to make one big word.
>
> every + one = **everyone**

A Write three compound words, each beginning with these words.

1 every _____ _____ _____

2 some _____ _____ _____

3 any _____ _____ _____

B Write three sentences. Each sentence must have two compound words.

1 _____

2 _____

3 _____

Punctuation

Commas in lists

> When we write a **list** in a sentence we use **commas** between the items in the list.
> We can join the last two things in the list with **and, but** and **or**.
>
> I like reading books about animals, plants **and** space.

A Write sentences of your own including these **lists**.

1 films   music   sport

_____

_____

2 dinosaurs   plants   electricity

_____

_____

3 birds   animals   science   mathematics   stars

_____

_____

Spelling

Prefixes

> A **prefix** is a group of letters added to the beginning of a word to change its meaning.
> Some prefixes give a word the **opposite** meaning.
>
> correct   **in**correct
>
> When a prefix is added to a word, don't worry if it doubles some letters.

A Underline the prefix in each of these words.

1 misfortune   2 dishonest   3 insensitive   4 distrust

5 impossible   6 illegible   7 invisible   8 irresponsible

B Write three words that begin with each of these prefixes.

Use a dictionary to help.

dis
_____
_____
_____

mis
_____
_____
_____

in
_____
_____
_____

im
_____
_____
_____

il
_____
_____
_____

ir
_____
_____
_____

C Add a prefix to each of these words to make a new word.

1 _____ obey

2 _____ lead

3 _____ correct

4 _____ perfect

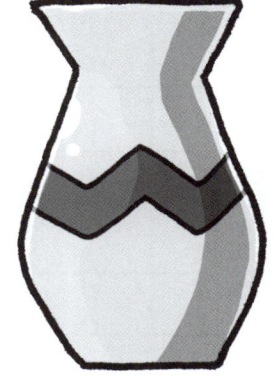

Grammar

Singular and plural nouns

> One is **singular**.
> More than one is **plural**.

We add **s** to lots of **naming words** when we mean **more than one**.

| one book | two book**s** | one torch | two torch**es** |
| one story | two stor**ies** | one boy | two boy**s** |

Nouns ending in **f** and **fe** can be made **plural** by changing the **f** or **fe** to **v** and adding **es**.

one shel**f**   two shel**ves**   one li**fe**   two li**ves**

Some **f/fe** words just add **s**. You just have to learn these.

cliff   cliffs   roof   roofs

A Write the **plural** of these nouns.
Put each **plural noun** into a sentence of your own.

1 leaf   plural: _____

Sentence: _____

_____

2 loaf   plural: _____

Sentence: _____

_____

3 roof   plural: _____

Sentence: _____

_____

B Write the **singular** of these nouns.
Put each **singular noun** into a sentence of your own.

1 wolves   singular: _____

Sentence: _____

_____

2 lives   singular: _____

Sentence: _____

_____

3 cliffs   singular: _____

Sentence: _____

_____

Writing

Using a library

A library is a good place to find story books and books with information and facts about different topics. Use this page to write information about using a library.

1 Write **three** things that you could use a library for.

_____

_____

_____

2 What is the difference between fiction and non-fiction books?

_____

_____

_____

3 Write **five** rules about using a library. You could write these as **dos** and **don'ts**.

_____

_____

_____

_____

_____

_____

_____

_____

_____

_____

UNIT 15 Sorry, Sorry, Sorry

Vocabulary

Synonyms

Remember, a **synonym** is a word with the same or a similar meaning to another word.

A Use a thesaurus to choose two synonyms for each of these words.

1. join _____ _____
2. bright _____ _____
3. strong _____ _____

B Write sentences using the synonyms you wrote in Activity A.

1. a _____
   b _____
2. a _____
   b _____
3. a _____
   b _____

Punctuation

Apostrophes

We use an **apostrophe** for:
1. **contractions**
   I **was**n't listening.   was**n't** = was not
2. **possessive nouns**
   the **alien's** planet = the planet belonging to the alien
   the **aliens'** planet = the planet belonging to the aliens

A Make **contractions** for the words below using an **apostrophe**.

1. do not _____   2. they are _____

B Write these as **possessive nouns** using an **apostrophe**.

1. the ship belonging to the pirate _____
2. the dreams belonging to the boys _____

Spelling

ei words

This unit covers the different sounds that the spelling pattern **ei** can make.
Say these words aloud:
   w**ei**ght   h**ei**ght   w**ei**rd
Can you hear the different sounds that the **ei** makes?

A Circle the words with the same **ei** sound as in **eight**.

weight	ceiling	eighty	vein
either	deceive	rein	receipt
freight	height	weird	their

B Write these words into your own sentence.
If you don't know what a word means, check it in a dictionary first.

1 eight _____

2 reins _____

3 height _____

4 ceiling _____

5 their _____

C Add **ei** or **eigh** to complete each of these words.

1 v_____n

2 w_____

3 _____teen

4 n_____bour

5 rec_____ve

6 w_____rdly

Grammar

Verbs: irregular past simple tense

To put a **verb** into the **past simple tense**, we usually add **ed** or **d** to the verb family name.

Verb family name	Past simple tense
to drift	drift**ed**
to hear	hear**d**

Some **verbs** do not follow this rule.

to say	sa**id**
to make	ma**de**
to grow	gr**ew**

A Underline the **past simple verb** in each sentence.

1 Someone spoke to me.

2 They said something important.

3 I dreamt about an amazing place.

B Complete the table.

Verb family name	Past simple tense
to bring	I
to swim	He
to sing	We
to grow	She

C Use these **past simple verbs** in sentences of you own.

1 thought _____

_____

2 taught _____

_____

3 caught _____

_____

Writing

Humorous poetry

You are going to write your own limerick.

1. Start by thinking of as many words as you can that rhyme with the word 'East'.

   _____
   _____
   _____

2. Now think of other pairs of rhyming words.

   _____
   _____
   _____

3. Choose your favourite words and complete the table, so that you have two words that rhyme with 'East' for lines 2 and 5 and two other rhyming words for lines 3 and 4.

Line	Rhyming word	Line	Rhyming word
1	East	3	
2		4	
5			

4. Now complete the rest of your limerick, using your rhyming words.

   There was a young man from the East

   Who thought _____

   When he _____

   He _____

   And _____

UNIT 16 All about Sport

Vocabulary

Alphabetical order

A All these words can be found in a book on sport. Organise these words under the correct subheadings as they would be found in the index.

hockey	bats	shoes	cricket	accuracy
football	speed	strength	gloves	basketball
balance	helmets	tennis	teamwork	racquets

Index subheadings		
Sports	Equipment	Skills

B Now list the words from **Activity A** under each subheading alphabetically.

Index subheadings		
Sports	Equipment	Skills

Punctuation

Capital letters, question marks and exclamation marks

> All **sentences** start with a **capital letter**.
> A **statement** ends with a **full stop**.
> A **question** ends with a **question mark**.
> An **exclamation** ends with an **exclamation mark**.

A 1 Write a **statement** about your favourite sport.

_____

2 Write a **question** about your favourite sport.

_____

3 Write an **exclamation** about your favourite sport.

_____

Spelling

Prefixes

> A **prefix** is a group of letters added to the beginning of a word to change its meaning.
> Remember, when a prefix is added to a word, don't worry if it doubles some letters.

A Complete these word sums.

1 non + sense = _____   2 de + code = _____

3 pre + view = _____   4 re + place = _____

5 un + cover = _____   6 de + bug = _____

B Sort the words with prefixes from **Activity A** into this table.

un	non	pre	re	de

C Fill the gaps in the table with more words with prefixes. You can use a dictionary to help.

Grammar

Abstract nouns

> There are different types of **nouns**.
> **Concrete nouns** are the names of things you can see and touch.
> **Abstract nouns** are the names of things you cannot touch, taste, smell or hear.

A Write each **noun** from the box under the correct heading.

success   ambition   snowboard   goalkeeper
equipment   fairness   Sunday   shoes
bravery   health   football   food

Concrete nouns	Abstract nouns

B Use these **abstract nouns** in sentences of your own.

1 skill _____

_____

2 speed _____

_____

3 opinion _____

_____

4 fitness _____

_____

_____

Writing

Indexes

You are going to write an **index** from a book called *The Planets*.

1 Read the names of the planets that go around the sun.

Mercury	Venus
Earth	Mars
Jupiter	Saturn
Uranus	Neptune

2 In the book, you can find information about the different planets on the following pages.

page 5: Earth, Mars	page 7: Saturn
page 8: Uranus	page 10: Mercury, Venus
page 15: Earth	page 17: Jupiter, Venus
page 18: Neptune	page 19: Mars
page 21: Saturn, Jupiter	page 22: Neptune

3 Make an index for the book. The first entry has been done to help you.

INDEX	Page number
Earth	5, 15

UNIT 17 Me and Mister P

Vocabulary

Words within words

A There are lots of words hidden in this word search. They go from top to bottom and from left to right. Draw a circle around each word you can find. Watch out, some have smaller words within them!

t	e	l	e	v	i	s	i	o	n
a	n	t	m	q	p	m	e	n	l
l	z	r	p	w	f	i	m	e	e
k	o	q	t	i	n	l	o	n	g
c	l	d	y	p	s	e	g	k	a
a	t	o	m	o	r	r	o	w	m
f	u	r	q	l	x	y	r	a	e
e	n	l	b	a	j	h	v	s	f
b	e	a	r	r	a	i	n	v	q
x	i	f	o	o	t	b	a	l	l

Punctuation

Direct speech

> **Direct speech** is when we write words that someone has said. We put " at the beginning of the spoken words and " at the end of the spoken words.
> Sometimes the **speaker's name** comes before the spoken words. We use a **comma** to separate the non-spoken and spoken words.

A Rewrite these sentences so the **speaker's name** comes **first**.

1 "I want to see what is going on!" said Arthur.

_____

2 "That's enough!" shouted Mum.

_____

Spelling

Tricky words

Some words are useful to know but can be tricky to learn because the letters or letter patterns make different sounds to those expected. This section focuses on some of them.

A Sort these words into the table. If you are unsure of any of the meanings, look them up in a dictionary.

brochure	chef	myth	parachute
tongue	crystal	catalogue	league
machine	pyramid	mystery	gym

y as in i (b<u>i</u>t)	**gue** as in g (goat)	**ch** as in sh (<u>sh</u>op)

B Match each picture with a word from the table.

1

2

3

_____ _____ _____

4

5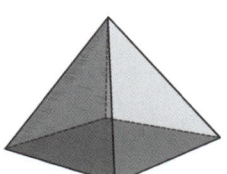

6

_____ _____ _____

Grammar

Pronouns

> A **pronoun** can be used instead of a **noun**.
> **Liam** watched television.   **He** watched television.
> **Mum** was cross.   **She** was cross.

A Underline the **pronoun** in each sentence.

1. I want to hear what's going on.
2. Arthur said he couldn't see the screen.
3. You have to try to understand.
4. We will not watch football today.
5. Was he imagining things?

B Rewrite each sentence, replacing the underlined words with **pronouns**.

1. <u>Liam</u> was sitting in front of the television.

   _____

2. <u>Mum</u> took the television control.

   _____

3. <u>Arthur and Liam</u> were not allowed to watch the football game.

   _____

4. <u>The polar bear</u> stood up on its back legs.

   _____

C Use these **pronouns** in sentences of your own.

1. I _____
2. You _____
3. He _____
4. She _____
5. It _____
6. We _____
7. They _____

How characters in stories make you feel

Use this page to help you write a description of a character from a story. You could invent your own character if you prefer.

The character I am writing about is called: _____

_____

To make the reader feel frightened, I would describe the character like this:

_____

_____

_____

_____

_____

To make the reader feel sad, I would describe the character like this:

_____

_____

_____

_____

_____

To make the reader laugh, I would describe the character like this:

_____

_____

_____

_____

_____

Book 3 Glossary

abstract noun a word that names something you cannot touch, taste, smell or hear – for example: *happiness*, *peace*

adjective (describing word) a word that tells us more about someone or something – for example: *loud*

adverb a word that tells us more about how something is done – for example: *loudly*

antonym words that have opposite meanings – for example: *happy/sad*; *fast/slow*

article words that come before a noun to tell you which person or thing the sentence is about – for example: *the*, *a*, *an*

comparative adjective a word that describes the difference between two things – for example: *longer*

compound word a word that is made by joining two words together – for example: *football*

concrete noun a word that names something you can touch, taste, smell or hear, opposite to an *abstract noun* – for example: *pen*, *book*

conjunction (joining word) a word used to join two sentences – for example: *and*

contents page the page at the beginning of a book that lists the topics or chapters in the book and their page numbers

contraction when a letter or letters are left out of a word, and replaced with an apostrophe – for example: *we're*

dialogue the words the characters say in a story, play or film

homonym words that sound the same and are spelt the same but have different meanings – for example: *bat* (*something used in sport and a flying animal*)

homophone words that sound the same, but are spelt differently and have a different meaning – for example: *son* and *sun*

possessive noun a noun that tells you who owns something using an apostrophe – for example: *Indre's book*

preposition a word that shows the relationship of a noun or pronoun to another word in the sentence – for example: *in*, *on*, *under*

pronoun a word that stands in place of a noun, used to avoid repeating the noun – for example: *he*, *them*, *it*

proper noun a noun that names a particular person, place or thing; proper nouns start with a capital letter – for example: *William*, *Australia*

synonym a word that has the same, or a similar meaning, as another word – for example: *big* and *large*

thesaurus a book that lists words in alphabetical order, with their synonyms and antonyms